CONTENTS

All meals serve four portions unless otherwise stated.

INTRODUCTION

If your idea of a quick meal is a ready-prepared frozen convenience food then think again. Even if your time in the kitchen is limited, you can still make nourishing meals from fresh ingredients. Many will be cheaper than those made from convenience foods and certainly all will be more interesting and appetising. With a skilful combination of good ingredients and quick methods of preparation and cooking, you should be able to make a three-course meal in under an hour.

Ingredients

Meat: If you wish to prepare a meal in a hurry using a conventional stove and no specialised equipment, do not buy large joints of meat or stewing cuts that will take a long time to cook. Choose instead the smaller, more tender cuts such as chops and cutlets, steaks, chicken drumsticks and offal meats. Minced beef is useful for making quickly prepared meals. Larger or less tender meats can be cooked in a microwave oven or a pressure cooker (see pages 50-63).

Fish: Most fish will cook quickly and so are highly suitable for making a quick meal. Fresh fish are more economical than frozen.

Eggs and Dairy Products: Eggs are the ideal ingredient with which to prepare a meal in a short time, whether they are boiled, scrambled, or cooked in a frying pan. Cheese, depending on which type you choose, can be used for main courses, first courses, or desserts, in dishes both hot and cold. Yoghurt is excellent for quick sauces and salad dressings and toppings for all types of desserts.

Pulses: Pulses, bought dried, take a long time to cook. However, you can buy many types ready-cooked and canned in lightly salted water. All you have to do is mix them with flavouring ingredients, salad dressings, or other vegetables, depending on the recipe directions.

Vegetables: Fresh vegetables are more nourishing and far more tasty than canned and frozen varieties. Choose those that require the minimum of preparation, such as cabbages that only need to be shredded or courgettes that can simply be sliced. Potatoes and root vegetables need not be peeled; simply give them a good scrub before slicing or chopping. Salads help to save even more time since no cooking is involved. They can be served as a first course, or they can accompany the main dish.

Fruit: Fresh fruit is always easy to use. Some types, such as melon or grapefruit, will make a first course in minutes; others can be made into fruit salads or quickly prepared hot fruit dishes.

Where fresh fruit is not available, or when you wish to prepare a dessert with the minimum of preparation, choose fruits that have been canned in natural juices. A wide range is now available from many supermarkets.

Fruit Juices: These make ideal first courses, either alone or mixed with other ingredients. They can also be used as an ingredient in desserts.

Pasta and Grains: Pasta will cook in twelve minutes and so is very useful in the quick cook's kitchen. Wholewheat pasta is used throughout the book for its extra nourishing qualities. Other grains that are quick to prepare include burghul wheat, millet and buckwheat, all of which can be bought in health food shops. Wherever rice is used in the following recipes, brown is specified. This takes about forty minutes to cook, but as long as it is put on to cook before the other parts of the meal are prepared, the meal will still be a quick one. If wished, white rice can be used, but this is not so healthy and has a poorer flavour. Rolled oats and crunchy oat and wheat cereals are useful for preparing quick desserts.

GAIL DUFF
QUICK MEALS

HAMLYN

First published in 1986 by
Hamlyn Publishing
Bridge House, London Road,
Twickenham, Middlesex, England

Copyright © Hamlyn Publishing, a division of
The Hamlyn Publishing Group Limited

Produced by New Leaf Productions

Photography by Mick Duff
Design by Jim Wire
Typeset by System Graphics Ltd., Folkestone
Series Editor: James M. Gibson

ISBN 0 600 32638 1

Printed in Spain

Lito. A. Romero, S. A. - D. L. TF. 755 – 1986

We would like to thank:
Jenny Hudson.
Mick Clarke, Honesty Wholefoods, Union St.,
Maidstone, Kent.
Lurcocks of Lenham, The Square, Lenham, Kent.
Brian Cook and Son, High St., Charing, Kent.
also:
Nasons of Canterbury for the loan of crockery,
tablecloths, napkins, etc.

Some cooking methods

The oven is used very little in the following recipes because of the length of time needed to get it up to temperature.

Grilling, stir-frying and sautéing are all quick methods by which to cook meat, offal and fish. When grilling, always heat the grill before putting the food underneath. This will ensure that it is cooked evenly and in as short a time as possible. When stir-frying, make sure that all the ingredients are chopped and prepared before you heat the oil or butter. This will prevent any last-minute panics. Sautéing usually involves quick frying first and then a longer simmering in a small amount of liquid. Make sure that the heat under the pan is as low as possible for the second stage of cooking to prevent drying or sticking.

Some of the recipes below involve mixing all the constituents of the meal into one big main dish. These include pasta dishes, main course salads, grain dishes and stuffed pancakes. Generally, the time involved in their preparation will be less than for several separate dishes brought together at the end.

Useful kitchen equipment

A grill pan, saucepans and a frying pan, plus a general supply of knives and spoons should be all that is needed to prepare most of the recipes in the following pages. However, a food processor or liquidiser is extremely useful for preparing drinks, soups and some desserts. A pressure cooker and a microwave oven have their own special uses; therefore, each has been allotted a separate recipe section.

Planning and preparing quick meals

When planning a complete meal, try to work out which ingredients or dishes will take longer to cook (for example brown rice) and start these cooking first. It saves time to prepare one set of ingredients while another part of the meal is cooking. When choosing a menu, choose some dishes that will need more chopping and preparing, such as salads and some that can simmer away by themselves for a while such as sauté dishes. In this way, you can work on several dishes at once.

COMPLETE QUICK MEALS

The recipes on the following pages are arranged in complete meals, giving a first course, main course with accompaniments and a dessert. This gives an idea of how quick meals can be planned. They can, of course, be intermixed according to personal taste, and some recipes can be made less complicated, for example, pasta, rice, or potatoes can be served plainly after having been boiled, instead of being mixed with flavouring ingredients.

> *Carrot and Orange Juice Whiz*
> *Rump Steak with Rice and Aubergines*
> *Two-Cress Salad*
> *Raspberry Crunch*

CARROT AND ORANGE JUICE WHIZ

425 ml/¾ pint natural orange juice
425 ml/¾ pint carrot juice
125 ml/4 fl oz natural yoghurt

Put all the ingredients into a blender or food processor until they make a smooth, frothy drink.

RUMP STEAK WITH RICE AND AUBERGINES

225 g/8 oz long-grain brown rice
675 g/1½ lb aubergines
1 tablespoon salt
675 g/1½ lb rump steak, cut about 1.5 cm/½ inch thick
4 tablespoons olive oil
2 medium onions, thinly sliced
1 clove garlic, finely chopped
4 tablespoons chopped parsley

Cook the rice in lightly salted boiling water for 40 minutes. Drain it, run cold water through it and drain it again. Meanwhile, cut the aubergines into 1.5-cm/½-inch cubes. Layer them in a collander with the salt. Leave them to drain for 15 minutes. Rinse them with cold water and dry them with kitchen paper. Cut the steak into 1.5-cm/½-inch cubes. Heat the oil in a large frying pan or paella pan on a high heat. Put

in the beef and stir it until all the pieces are well browned. Lower the heat and mix in the aubergines, onions and garlic. Cook for 10 minutes, stirring frequently until the onions are soft and the aubergines have a soft, melting texture. Put the beef and aubergines into a serving dish. Raise the heat under the pan. Put in the rice and stir it on the heat for 1 minute. Mix in the parsley. Either put the rice into a separate dish or arrange it round the beef and aubergines.

TWO-CRESS SALAD

100 g/4 oz watercress
2 boxes mustard and cress
4 tablespoons olive or sunflower oil
juice of ½ lemon
1 teaspoon Dijon mustard
1 clove garlic, crushed

Chop the watercress and put it into a bowl. Cut the mustard and cress from the boxes and add it to the watercress. Beat the remaining ingredients together to make the dressing and fold it into the salad.

RASPBERRY CRUNCH

350 g/12 oz raspberries, fresh or frozen
2 tablespoons clear honey
175 g/6 oz wheatflake breakfast cereal with
   dried fruits and nuts
150 ml/¼ pint double cream
150 ml/¼ pint Greek-style yoghurt
2 tablespoons chopped walnuts

Mix the raspberries with the honey and leave them for 10 minutes. Put the breakfast cereal into the bottom of a serving dish. Stiffly whip the cream and fold in the yoghurt. Arrange the raspberries on top of the cereal and cover them with the cream and yoghurt mixture. Scatter the walnuts over the top.

> *Celery and Walnut Salads*
> *Quick-Fried Minced Beef with Red Peppers*
> *Tagliatelle with Parsley*
> *Banana and Kiwi Fruit Cheesecakes*

CELERY AND WALNUT SALADS

6 celery sticks
50 g/2 oz walnuts, chopped
2 tablespoons sunflower oil
1 tablespoon cider vinegar
1 clove garlic, crushed
freshly ground black pepper
4 tablespoons thick yoghurt
4 walnut halves

Chop the celery. Put it into a bowl with the chopped walnuts. Beat together the oil, vinegar, garlic and pepper. Fold the resulting dressing into the celery and walnuts. Divide the salad between four small bowls. Put a portion of the yoghurt on top and garnish each salad with a walnut half.

QUICK-FRIED MINCED BEEF WITH RED PEPPERS

675 g/1½ lb minced beef
2 large red peppers
1 large onion
1 tablespoon sunflower oil
2 cloves garlic, finely chopped
2 tablespoons chopped parsley
1 tablespoon marjoram or 1 teaspoon dried
1 tablespoon chopped thyme or 1 teaspoon dried

Core, seed and finely chop the peppers. Finely chop the onion. Heat the oil in a large, heavy frying pan on a high heat. Put in the beef, break it up well and stir it around until it begins to brown. Mix in the peppers, onion, garlic and herbs and keep stirring on a high heat for 2 minutes. Lower the heat and cook for a further 5 minutes, stirring occasionally until the meat is completely cooked and the peppers slightly crisp.

TAGLIATELLE WITH PARSLEY

225 g/8 oz wholewheat tagliatelle
3 tablespoons olive oil
1 clove garlic, crushed
25 g/1 oz parsley, finely chopped

Cook the tagliatelle in lightly salted boiling water for 12 minutes or until it is just tender. Drain it, rinse it with cold water and drain it again. Put the oil and garlic into a saucepan and heat them on a medium heat until the garlic begins to sizzle. Stir in the tagliatelle and heat it through. Fold in the parsley.

BANANA AND KIWI FRUIT CHEESECAKES

100 g/4 oz digestive biscuits
50 g/2 oz butter
2 bananas
2 kiwi fruit
100 g/4 oz low-fat soft cheese or cream cheese
juice of ½ lemon

Crush the digestive biscuits or work them in a blender or food processor to make fine crumbs. Put them into a bowl. Melt the butter, without letting it foam. Add it to the biscuit crumbs and mix well. Put the mixture into four flat-based glass dishes or one 20-cm/8-inch diameter tart dish. Chill it while you prepare the topping. Peel 1 banana and 1 kiwi fruit. Either put them into a blender or food processor with the cheese and lemon juice and work them to a smooth purée; or mash them and rub them through a sieve before beating them gradually into the cheese and adding the lemon juice. Put the mixture on top of the buttered crumbs. Peel the remaining banana and kiwi fruit. Slice them and use them as a garnish.

> *Tomato Toasts*
> *Lamb Chops with Oranges*
> *Potatoes Steamed with Celery*
> *Grape Jellies*

TOMATO TOASTS

4 tomatoes
25 g/1 oz butter
1 tablespoon tomato purée
2 slices from a large wholemeal loaf
½ teaspoon dried thyme
2 anchovy fillets

Cut each tomato in half crosswise. Cream the butter with the tomato purée. Cut each slice of bread into quarters. Toast them on one side only. Turn them over and spread the untoasted side with the flavoured butter. Put a tomato half onto each piece of toast. Sprinkle it with a little thyme. Cut each anchovy into four and lay a piece on each tomato half. Return the toast to the grill for 2 minutes until the tomatoes are heated through and the anchovies sizzling.

LAMB CHOPS WITH ORANGES

8 small, lean lamb chops
2 small, sharp oranges
15 g/½ oz butter
1 small onion, thinly sliced
200 ml/7 fl oz stock
2 tablespoons chopped or 1 tablespoon dried
    lemon thyme (use ordinary thyme if no
    lemon thyme is available)
¼ teaspoon cayenne

Trim any excess fat from the chops. Cut a thin slice from the top and bottom of each orange and discard it. Cut each orange into four slices. Melt the butter in a large frying pan on a high heat. Put in the chops, brown them on both sides and remove them. Lower the heat, put in the onion and soften it. Pour in the stock and bring it to the boil. Add the lemon thyme and cayenne and replace the chops. Cover and cook on a low heat for 15 minutes. Turn the chops and put a slice of orange on each one. Cover again and cook for a further 15 minutes. Serve the chops with the orange slices still on top and any remaining sauce spooned round them.

POTATOES STEAMED WITH CELERY

675 g/1½ lb small potatoes
1 head celery
1 large onion
¼ nutmeg, grated or ¼ teaspoon ground
  nutmeg
freshly ground black pepper

Scrub and thinly slice the potatoes. There is no need to peel them. Cut the celery into 2-cm/¾-inch pieces. Thinly slice the onion. Put them all into a large vegetable steamer or collander. Season them with the nutmeg and plenty of pepper. Bring a large pan of water to the boil. Set the steamer or collander over the top. Cover with a lid or foil. Steam for 25 minutes, turning once. The vegetables should be tender but firm enough to hold their shape.

GRAPE JELLIES

450 g/1 lb black grapes
grated rind of 1 orange
575 ml/1 pint grape juice
agar-agar to set 575 ml/1 pint liquid (see
  manufacturer's instructions)★
whipped cream or natural yoghurt (optional)

Halve and seed the grapes. Mix them with the orange rind. Either divide them between four small glass bowls or put them into one large one. Put the grape juice into a bowl. Bring it almost to boiling point. Stir in the agar-agar and stir until it has dissolved. Take the pan from the heat. Cool the juice a little and pour it over the grapes. Put the jelly into the refrigerator for 30 minutes to set. Serve topped with whipped cream or thick yoghurt if wished.

★Agar-agar is a vegetarian gelling agent which sets jellies far quicker than gelatin. It can be bought either in crystal or powder form. The amounts needed for the two types vary, so always consult the packet instructions.

Lambs' Kidneys with Mushrooms
Herby Rice
Calabrese with Parmesan
Cheese and Chicory Salad

LAMBS' KIDNEYS WITH MUSHROOMS

12 lambs' kidneys
225 g/8 oz button mushrooms
25 g/1 oz butter
1 medium onion, finely chopped
1 clove garlic. finely chopped
150 ml/¼ pint stock
grated rind and juice of 1 lemon
1 tablespoon Worcestershire sauce
1 tablespoon tomato purée
4 tablespoons chopped parsley

Skin the kidneys. Cut them in half crossways and snip out the cores. Thinly slice the mushrooms. Melt the butter in a frying pan on a high heat. Put in the kidneys, onion and garlic and move them around on the heat until the kidneys have browned. Mix in the mushrooms. Pour in the stock and bring it to the boil. Add the lemon rind and juice, Worcestershire sauce and tomato purée. Lower the heat to a simmer. Cook, uncovered, for 5 minutes. Serve sprinkled with parsley in the centre of a bed of rice.

HERBY RICE

225 g/8 oz long-grain brown rice
2 teaspoons dried mixed herbs
575 ml/1 pint stock

Put the rice, herbs and stock into a saucepan. Bring them to the boil. Cover and cook on a low heat for 40 minutes or until all the stock has been absorbed and the rice is tender.

CALABRESE WITH PARMESAN

675 g/½ lb calabrese
25 g/1 oz butter
2 tablespoons grated Parmesan cheese

Trim the calabrese. Steam it for 20 minutes or until it is tender. Put it into a serving dish. Melt the butter in a frying pan on a medium heat. Sprinkle in the Parmesan cheese and cook it until it is just beginning to brown. Spoon the mixture over the calabrese.

CHEESE AND CHICORY SALAD

4 small bulbs chicory
1 tablespoon sesame seeds
4 tablespoons sesame or sunflower oil
1 tablespoon freshly squeezed orange juice
1 tablespoon white wine vinegar
pinch of cayenne
8 long strips yellow or red pepper
100 g/4 oz goat's cheese, Melbury or Brie

Cut each bulb of chicory in half lengthwise. Lay the halves one each side of four small plates. Put the sesame seeds into a heavy frying pan. Set them on a medium heat without any fat or oil. Stir them until they brown and smell nutty. Tip them onto a plate to cool. Beat together the oil, orange juice and vinegar. Spoon the liquid over the chicory. Sprinkle the chicory with the cayenne and the sesame seeds. Put a strip of pepper on each piece of chicory. Thinly slice the cheese. Lay the slices between the pieces of chicory.

Chickpea and Green Olive Salad
Pork Chops with Clove, Mustard and Apples
Carrots with Marjoram
Potatoes with Mustard and Cress
Pineapple, Orange and Prune Cup

CHICKPEA AND GREEN OLIVE SALAD

175 g/6 oz drained canned chickpeas
6 green olives, stoned and quartered
4 tablespoons chopped parsley
2 tablespoons sunflower oil
1 tablespoon white wine vinegar
1 clove garlic, crushed
freshly ground black pepper
4 parsley sprigs

Mix together the chickpeas, olives and parsley. Beat together the oil, vinegar, garlic and pepper and fold them into the chickpeas. Divide the salad between four small plates or bowls. Garnish with the parsley.

PORK CHOPS WITH CLOVE, MUSTARD AND APPLES

4 loin pork chops
1 tablespoon mustard powder
½ teaspoon ground cloves
2 teaspoons dried sage
1 tablespoon dry cider
1 large Bramley apple
2 tablespoons sunflower oil

Cut the rind and any excess fat from the chops. Mix together the mustard powder, half the cloves, the sage and cider. Spread half the mixture over one side of the chops. Peel and core the apple and cut it into twelve lengthwise slices. Put the oil into a bowl and turn the apple slices in it. Heat the grill to high. Lay the chops on the hot rack, mustard side up. Grill them for 7 minutes or until browned on that side. Turn the chops over and spread them with the remaining mustard mixture. Grill them for a further 7 minutes or until they are well browned and cooked through. Lay three apple slices on each chop and sprinkle them with the remaining cloves. Return the chops to the grill for a further 2 minutes for the apples to heat through and begin to soften.

CARROTS WITH MARJORAM

675 g/½ lb carrots
25 g/1 oz butter or vegetable margarine
425 ml/¾ pint water
1 teaspoon dried marjoram

Slice the carrots. Put all the ingredients into a saucepan. Bring them to the boil. Cover and cook on a medium heat for 15 minutes, or until the carrots are just tender and all the liquid has been absorbed.

POTATOES WITH MUSTARD AND CRESS

675–900 g/1½–2 lb potatoes
25 g/1 oz butter or vegetable margarine
2 boxes mustard and cress

Scrub the potatoes. Boil them in their skins until they are just tender. Drain them. Slice them as soon as they are cool enough to handle. Melt the butter in a saucepan on a medium heat. Fold in the sliced potatoes and mustard and cress. Heat them through for 1 minute.

PINEAPPLE, ORANGE AND PRUNE CUP

1 medium pineapple
2 medium oranges
one 425-g/15-oz can prunes in natural juice
4 tablespoons rum

Cut the husk from the pineapple. Cut the flesh into 1.5-cm/½-inch slices. Cut out the cores and cut the slices into small sections. Cut the rind and pith from the oranges. Cut the flesh into lengthwise quarters. Thinly slice the quarters. Drain the prunes, reserving the juice. Halve and pit them. In a serving bowl, mix together the pineapple, oranges and prunes. Mix in the rum and 4 tablespoons of the reserved juice.

Creamy Carrot Soup
Stir-braised Pork with Herbs and Spices
Potatoes with Parsley
Green Cabbage and Green Peppers
Fruity Coconut Yoghurt

CREAMY CARROT SOUP

425 ml/¾ pint carrot juice
425 ml/¾ pint full cream milk
175 g/6 oz carrots, finely grated
100 g/4 oz curd or cream cheese

Put the carrot juice, milk and grated carrots into a saucepan. Heat them to just below boiling point. Pour the soup into individual bowls. Float a portion of cheese on the top of each one.

STIR-BRAISED PORK WITH HERBS AND SPICES

900 g/2 lb lean pork (shoulder or spare rib)
½ teaspoon black peppercorns
½ teaspoon juniper berries
½ teaspoon allspice berries
pinch of salt
15 g/½ oz butter (if necessary)
2 teaspoons chopped rosemary or 1 teaspoon
    dried
2 sage leaves, chopped or ¼ teaspoon dried
200 ml/7 fl oz dry white wine (stock or dry
    cider may be used if wine is not available

Cut the pork into 2-cm/¾-inch pieces. Crush the spices and salt together. Heat a large, heavy frying pan on a high heat. Put in the pork and stir it about until it browns. After a time, it should make enough of its own fat, but if the pan still looks dry after about 2 minutes, add the butter. Mix in the crushed spices and herbs. Pour in the wine and bring it to the boil. Cover the pan and keep it on a low heat for 30 minutes.

POTATOES WITH PARSLEY

675 g/1½ lb potatoes
25 g/1 oz butter
4 tablespoons chopped parsley

Scrub the potatoes. New potatoes work well and if using these, leave them whole. Cut larger ones into approximately 5-cm/2-inch pieces. Boil the potatoes in their skins until they are just tender. Drain them. Melt the butter in the saucepan on a low heat. Put in the potatoes and parsley and toss them in the butter.

GREEN CABBAGE AND GREEN PEPPERS

1 small green cabbage
2 green peppers
1 small onion
25 g/l oz butter
90 ml/3 fl oz water

Shred the cabbage. Core and seed the peppers and cut them into strips about 6-mm × 2.5-cm/¼ × 1-inch. Thinly slice the onion. Melt the butter in a saucepan on a high heat. Stir in the cabbage, peppers and onion. Pour in the water and bring it to the boil. Cover and cook on a low heat for 15 minutes. Drain if necessary, before serving.

FRUITY COCONUT YOGHURT

425-g/15-oz can fruit cocktail in natural juice
275 ml/1½ pint Greek-style natural yoghurt
75 g/3 oz dessicated coconut

Drain the fruits. Mix them into the yoghurt, together with the coconut. Let stand for 30 minutes before serving.

Avocado filled with Mushrooms
Sage and Onion Drumsticks
Root Vegetable Champ
Banana and Almond Syllabub

AVOCADO FILLED WITH MUSHROOMS

2 ripe avocados
100 g/4 oz button mushrooms
4 tablespoons olive or sunflower oil
juice of 1 lemon
1 tablespoon tomato purée
4 parsley sprigs

Halve and pit the avocados. Thinly slice the mushrooms. Beat the remaining ingredients together. Mix in the mushrooms. Put each avocado half onto a separate dish. Fill it with the mushroom salad.

SAGE AND ONION DRUMSTICKS

8 chicken drumsticks
25 g/1 oz wholewheat flour
1 medium onion
15 g/½ oz butter
1 tablespoon sunflower oil
200 ml/7 fl oz stock
2 tablespoons sage and onion mustard
4 tablespoons chopped parsley

Coat the drumsticks in the flour. Finely chop the onion. Heat the butter and oil together in a frying pan or sauté pan on a medium heat. Put in the drumsticks, brown them and remove them. Lower the heat. Put in the onion and soften it. Pour in the stock and bring it to the boil. Stir in the mustard. Return the drumsticks to the pan. Cover and cook on a low heat for 20 minutes or until the drumsticks are tender. Serve scattered with the parsley.

ROOT VEGETABLE CHAMP

450 g/1 lb potatoes
450 g/1 lb parsnips
350 g/12 oz carrots
225 g/8 oz white turnips
50 g/2 oz butter
4 tablespoons chopped parsley

Peel the potatoes and cut them into chunks. Scrub and core the parsnips and cut them into chunks. Scrub and slice the carrots and turnips. Bring a large pan of lightly salted water to the boil. Put in all the vegetables. Cover and cook for 20 minutes. Drain the vegetables. Mash them together or purée them in a blender or food processor. Put them into a serving dish. Make a small well in the centre and put in the butter. Scatter the parsley round the edge.

BANANA AND ALMOND SYLLABUB

275 ml/½ pint double cream
grated rind of 1 orange
4 tablespoons of brandy
2 bananas
50 g/2 oz ground almonds
50 g/2 oz flaked almonds

Stiffly whip the cream. Mix in the orange rind and brandy. Either chop the bananas and work them in a blender or food processor to a purée; or mash them and rub them through a sieve. Mix them into the cream. Mix in the ground almonds. Lightly toast the flaked almonds. Mix all but 2 tablespoons into the syllabub. Divide the syllabub between four individual glasses or bowls. Scatter the remaining almond flakes over the top.

TOMATO AND EGG-FLOWER SOUP

450 g/1 lb tomatoes
2 medium onions
3 tablespoons sunflower oil
850 ml/1½ pints stock
4 tablespoons soy sauce
2 eggs, beaten

Cut each tomato into eight lengthways slices. Halve the onions and cut them into thin, crescent-shaped pieces. Heat the oil in a saucepan on a low heat. Put in the onions and soften them. Put in the tomatoes and cook them, stirring frequently, for 2 minutes. Pour in the stock and bring it to the boil. Add the soy sauce. Add the eggs in a thin stream, pouring them over the prongs of a fork. Stir until they have set in thin strands.

STIR-FRIED TURKEY BREASTS WITH BEAN SPROUTS

675 g/1½ lb turkey breasts
175 g/6 oz bean sprouts
1 tablespoon cornflour
90 ml/3 fl oz stock
90 ml/3 fl oz dry sherry
1 tablespoon soy sauce
4 tablespoons sunflower or peanut oil
1 clove garlic, finely chopped

Cut the turkey breasts into small, thin slivers. Put them into a bowl and mix in the cornflour. Mix together the stock, sherry and soy sauce. Heat the oil in a large frying pan or wok on a high heat. Put in the turkey and stir it around until all the pieces have cooked to a white colour. Put in the bean sprouts and garlic and continue cooking and stirring for 1 minute. Pour in the stock mixture. Bring it to the boil. Cover and simmer for 15 minutes.

SOY RICE WITH MIXED VEGETABLES

225 g/8 oz long-grain brown rice
3 tablespoons sunflower oil
1 medium onion, finely chopped
1 clove garlic, finely chopped
1 teaspoon ground ginger
575 ml/1 pint stock
4 tablespoons soy sauce
1 green pepper
1 red pepper
one 225-g/8-oz can water chestnuts

Heat the oil in a saucepan on a low heat. Stir in the rice, onion, garlic and ginger. Pour in the stock and bring it to the boil. Add the soy sauce. Cover and cook for 25 minutes. Core, seed and dice the peppers. Drain and thinly slice the water chestnuts. Add them to the rice. Continue cooking for a further 15 minutes.

BRANDIED STRAWBERRY BRULÉE

450 g/1 lb strawberries, fresh or frozen
3 tablespoons brandy
100 g/4 oz crunchy oat cereal
150 ml/¼ pint soured cream
2 tablespoons Barbados sugar

Put one third of the strawberries into a high-sided, flameproof dish, such as a soufflé dish. Sprinkle in 1 tablespoon brandy and cover them with one-third of the cereal. Repeat the layers twice. Lightly beat the soured cream and then spoon it over the final layer of cereal. Scatter the sugar over the top. Leave until you are almost ready to serve. Heat the grill to high. Put the dish under the grill for the sugar to caramelise, about 5 minutes. Serve immediately, to achieve a hot and cold effect.

Pineapple Crush
Grilled Trout with Horseradish
Cinnamon-flavoured Salad
Potatoes with Sage and Onions
Chestnut Whip

GRILLED TROUT WITH HORSERADISH

4 medium trout
3 tablespoons grated horseradish
4 tablespoons chopped parsley
25 g/1 oz butter
juice of 1 lemon

Have the trout cleaned when you buy them, leaving the heads on. Cut their tails into neat V-shapes. Make three diagonal slits on each side of the fish, running backwards and downwards from head to tail. Mix together the horseradish and parsley. Push the mixture into the slits in the trout. Put the butter and lemon juice into a small pan. Set them on a low heat until the butter has melted. Brush the mixture over the trout, making sure that it goes in the slits. Heat the grill to high and, if you have an open wire rack, cover it with foil. Lay the trout on the hot rack and grill them for about 5 minutes on each side, or until they are browned and cooked through.

PINEAPPLE CRUSH

575 ml/1 pint orange and passion fruit juice★
325 ml/12 fl oz pineapple juice
4 slices fresh pineapple or pineapple canned in
natural juice

Put the fruit juices and the chopped pineapple into a blender or food processor. Work to a smooth, frothy, refreshing drink.

★Orange and passion fruit juice can be bought in some supermarkets. If it is not available, natural orange juice can be used instead.

CINNAMON-FLAVOURED SALAD

½ small white cabbage
2 large carrots
1 cooking apple
4 tablespoons sunflower oil
2 tablespoons cider vinegar
1 teaspoon ground cinnamon
1 clove garlic, crushed
freshly ground black pepper

Shred the cabbage. Grate the carrots. Core and chop the apple. Put them into a bowl. Beat the remaining ingredients together to make the dressing and fold it into the salad.

POTATOES WITH SAGE AND ONIONS

675–900 g/1½–2 lb potatoes
8 spring onions
25 g/1 oz butter
4 sage leaves, finely chopped or ½ teaspoon
   dried sage
freshly ground black pepper

Boil the potatoes in their skins until they are just tender. Drain and slice them. Chop the spring onions. Melt the butter in a saucepan on a low heat. Add the spring onions and sage. Fold in the potatoes. Stir gently for 30 seconds to reheat. Season with the pepper.

CHESTNUT WHIP

one 439-g/15.5-oz can chestnut purée
2 tablespoons apricot jam, no–sugar–added if
   possible
4 tablespoons honey
100 g/4 oz fromage frais
angelica and glacé cherries for garnish

Either put all the ingredients into a blender or food processor and work them to a purée; or beat them together to make a smooth mixture. Put the whip into one large or four small dishes and garnish with pieces of angelica and glacé cherries.

Melon with Curd Cheese and Hazelnuts
Plaice with Orange and Capers
Tomatoes Simmered with Herbs
Deep Fried Potato Slices
Grilled Apple Crumble

MELON WITH CURD CHEESE AND HAZELNUTS

1 large honeydew melon
175 g/6 oz curd cheese
50 g/2 oz hazelnuts

Quarter the melon and scoop out the seeds. Fill the centres with the cheese. Arrange the hazelnuts on top.

PLAICE WITH ORANGE AND CAPERS

8 small or 4 large plaice fillets (total weight about 675 g/1½ lb)
25 g/1 oz butter
grated rind and juice of 1 medium orange
1 tablespoon mild spiced granular mustard
2 tablespoons chopped capers

If the fillets are large, cut them in half lengthways. Heat the grill to high. Put the butter either into the grill pan or into a large shallow flameproof dish. Put it under the grill to melt. Stir in the orange rind and juice and the mustard. Turn the fish fillets in the hot mixture, leaving them skin side down. Scatter the capers over the top. Put the fish under the grill for 6 minutes, or until it is cooked through and golden coloured.

TOMATOES SIMMERED WITH HERBS

12 small, firm tomatoes
25 g/1 oz butter
½ teaspoon dried thyme
½ teaspoon dried marjoram

Put the tomatoes into a bowl. Pour boiling water over them and leave them for 2 minutes. Peel away the skins. Melt the butter in a saucepan on a low heat. Put in the tomatoes and turn them in the butter. Sprinkle in the herbs. Cover and cook gently for 5 minutes, turning the tomatoes once.

DEEP FRIED POTATO SLICES

4 medium sized potatoes
oil for deep frying

Scrub the potatoes. Peel them if wished, but it is not necessary. Cut them into 6-mm/¼-inch thick slices. Heat a pan of deep oil to 170°C/325°F. Put in the potatoes and cook them for 2 minutes, or until they are cooked but not browned. Take out the potatoes and drain them on absorbent kitchen paper. Heat the oil to 190°C/375°F. Put in the potatoes and fry them until they are browned, Drain them on kitchen paper and serve them as soon as possible.

GRILLED APPLE CRUMBLE

450 g/1 lb cooking apples
2 tablespoons clear honey
¼ teaspoon ground cloves
75 g/3 oz porridge oats
25 g/1 oz chopped toasted hazelnuts
2 tablespoons sesame seeds
25 g/1 oz sunflower seeds
3 tablespoons sunflower oil
2 tablespoons Barbados sugar

Peel, core and slice the apples. Put them into a flat flameproof dish and mix in the honey and cloves. Mix together all the remaining ingredients. Heat the grill to high. Put the apples under the grill. Cook them for 2 minutes. Turn them and cook for a further 2 minutes. Scatter the oat mixture over the top. Return the dish to the grill for 3–4 minutes or until the oat mixture has browned on top. Serve hot or warm.

GRAPEFRUIT WITH BANANA DRESSING

4 small pink grapefruit
2 large bananas
2 tablespoons tahini★
juice of 1 lemon
1 clove garlic, crushed
freshly ground black pepper
8 black grapes

Cut the rind and pith from the grapefruit. Cut each fruit into four thick slices. Arrange them in an overlapping line on each of four small plates. Mash the bananas and work in the tahini, lemon juice, garlic and pepper. Spoon the mixture over the grapefruit. Halve and seed the grapes and use them as a garnish.

★Tahini is a paste made from ground sesame seeds. It can be bought from health food shops.

HOT HERRING AND KIPPER SALAD

2 medium herrings
350 g/12 oz kipper fillets
6 celery sticks
2 tablespoons white wine vinegar
2 teaspoons Dijon mustard
4 tablespoons sunflower oil
1 clove garlic, finely chopped
2 large, pickled Hungarian gherkins, finely chopped

Fillet the herrings and cut each fillet crosswise into 6-mm/¼-inch strips. Skin the kipper fillets and cut them into 6-mm/¼-inch strips. Finely chop the celery. Mix the vinegar and mustard together. Put the oil and garlic into a large frying pan and set them on a high heat. As soon as the garlic begins to sizzle, mix in the celery and stir for 2 minutes. Put in the herring and kipper pieces. Continue stirring for a further 2 minutes. The fish pieces should cook

through but not break up. Put in the gherkins. Pour in the vinegar and mustard mixture. Let it bubble. Lightly mix the fish and remove it from the heat. Serve as soon as possible.

PASTA WITH BEANS AND CORN

225 g/8 oz French beans
225 g/8 oz wholewheat pasta shapes
3 tablespoons olive or sunflower oil
1 tablespoon chopped thyme or 1 teaspoon dried
one 350-g/12-oz can sweetcorn kernels

Top and tail the beans and break them into short lengths. Boil the pasta and beans together in lightly salted water for 12 minutes or until they are just tender. Drain them. Heat the oil in the saucepan on a medium heat. Put in the pasta and beans, corn and thyme. Stir to heat through.

CHEESE CRACKERS

8 wholewheat crackers
4 individual portions Camembert
8 stuffed olives
1 large celery stick
8 stuffed olives
32 very small parsley sprigs
4 small celery sticks, with leaves if possible

Cut each portion of Camembert into eight thin slices. Arrange three on each cracker. Thinly slice the olives and lay them beside the Camembert slices. Cut the large celery stick into matchstick pieces. Lay them on the Camembert. Garnish with the parsley sprigs. Put two crackers onto each of four small plates. Lay a small celery stick beside them.

Finely chop the celery, apple and the walnuts. Mix together the vinegar, mustard and sage. Heat the oil in a frying pan on a high heat. Put in the celery, apple and garlic and stir-fry them for 1 minute. Put in the walnuts and stir-fry for 1 minute more. Pour in the vinegar mixture and let it bubble. Spoon the salad into four small bowls.

> *Hot Celery, Apple and Walnut Salad*
> *Millet with Peppers and Tomatoes*
> *Chickpeas, Smoked Mackerel*
> *and Sausage*
> *Orange with Orangerulle Cheese*

HOT CELERY, APPLE AND WALNUT SALAD

6 large celery sticks
1 large cooking apple
100 g/4 oz shelled walnuts
2 tablespoons cider vinegar
1 teaspoon mustard powder
4 chopped sage leaves or ½ teaspoon dried sage
3 tablespoons sunflower oil
1 clove garlic, finely chopped

MILLET WITH PEPPERS AND TOMATOES

225 g/8 oz millet
1 medium onion
4 tablespoons sunflower oil
1 clove garlic, chopped
575 ml/1 pint stock
pinch of cayenne
1 tablespoon tomato purée
1 green pepper
1 red pepper
350 g/12 oz tomatoes

Finely chop the onion. Heat the oil in a frying pan on a low heat. Put in the onion and garlic and cook them for 1 minute. Stir in the millet. Pour in the stock and bring it to the boil. Add the cayenne and tomato purée. Cover and cook on a low heat for 20 minutes or until all the stock has been absorbed and the millet is soft and fluffy. Core and chop the peppers. Slice the tomatoes. Mix them into the cooked millet. Cover the pan and take it off the heat. Leave it for 5 minutes. The peppers and tomatoes should heat through but remain crisp.

CHICKPEAS, SMOKED MACKEREL AND SAUSAGE

one 400-g/14-oz can chickpeas
225 g/8 oz boiling sausage★
2 smoked mackerel fillets
4 tablespoons sunflower or olive oil
1 large onion, thinly sliced
1 teaspoon paprika
¼ teaspoon cayenne
juice of 1 lemon
3 tablespoons chopped parsley

Drain the chickpeas. Dice the boiling sausage. Skin the mackerel fillets and cut them into 2-cm/¾-inch squares. Heat the oil in a frying pan on a low heat. Mix in the onion and cook it until it begins to soften. Mix in the sausage, chickpeas, paprika and cayenne and cook until the onion is just beginning to brown. Mix in the mackerel and heat it through. Pour in the lemon juice and let it bubble. Add the parsley.

★Boiling sausage can be bought in 225-g/8-oz horseshoe shapes that are usually vacuum-packed.

ORANGE WITH ORANGERULLE CHEESE

4 medium oranges
1 pack Orangerulle cheese★
2 tablespoons chopped toasted hazelnuts
4 hazelnuts

Cut the rind and pith from the oranges. Cut the flesh into halves lengthways. Thinly slice the halves. Arrange the slices round the edge of four small plates. Cut the cheese into sixteen thin slices. Arrange four in the centre of the oranges on each plate. Top them with a hazelnut. Scatter the chopped toasted hazelnuts over the orange slices.

★Orangerulle cheese is a cream cheese, flavoured with Grand Marnier and comes in a hazelnut-coated roll.

> *Grilled Celery with Stilton Cheese*
> *Eggs Simmered with Ham and Peppers*
> *Spaghetti with Mushrooms*
> *Stuffed Pears*

GRILLED CELERY WITH STILTON CHEESE

4 wide celery sticks
175 g/6 oz Stilton cheese
12 small parsley sprigs

Cut each celery stick into three pieces. Finely chop or grate the Stilton and pack it into the hollows in the sticks. Heat the grill to high. Grill the celery for 2 minutes, or until the Stilton is melted and bubbly. Garnish each piece of celery with a parsley sprig before serving.

EGGS SIMMERED WITH HAM AND PEPPERS

4 eggs
175 g/6 oz cooked lean ham
1 large red pepper
1 large green pepper
225 g/8 oz tomatoes
4 tablespoons olive oil
1 large onion, finely chopped
1 clove garlic, finely chopped
1 tablespoon chopped thyme

Finely dice the ham. Core, seed and finely chop the peppers. Scald, skin and chop the tomatoes. Heat the oil in a large frying pan on a high heat. Put in the onion and garlic and cook them for 2 minutes. Mix in the peppers, cover, and cook for 10 minutes. Mix in the tomatoes, ham and thyme. Cover again and cook for 5 minutes. Make four indentations in the mixture with the back of a spoon. Break in the eggs. Cover the pan and cook for 3 minutes until the whites of the eggs are set but the yolks are partially runny. Serve straight from the pan.

SPAGHETTI WITH MUSHROOMS

225 g/8 oz wholewheat spaghetti
100 g/4 oz mushrooms
3 tablespoons olive or sunflower oil
4 tablespoons chopped parsley
2 tablespoons grated Parmesan cheese

Cook the spaghetti in lightly salted boiling water for 12 minutes or until it is just tender. Drain it, run cold water through it and drain it again. Thinly slice the mushrooms. Heat the oil in a saucepan on a low heat. Put in the mushrooms and cook them for 1 minute, stirring occasionally. Fold in the spaghetti, parsley and Parmesan cheese. Heat through, if necessary.

STUFFED PEARS

2 ripe Comice pears, or large Conference pears
90 ml/3 fl oz Greek-style natural yoghurt
4 tablespoons no-sugar-added strawberry jam

Halve the pears. Using a teaspoon, scoop out and discard the cores. Scoop out most of the flesh to leave shells about 1-cm/⅜-inch thick. Chop the scooped-out pieces of pear. Mix together the yoghurt and 2 tablespoons of the jam. Mix in the chopped pear. Fill the pear shells with the mixture. Top them with a portion of jam.

Tomato and Bean Soup
Courgette Scramble
Anchovy Oatcakes with
Black Grapes

TOMATO AND BEAN SOUP

one 400-g/14-oz can tomatoes in juice
275 ml/½ pint tomato and vegetable juice
one 400-g/14-oz can butter beans or cannellini
  beans, drained
225 g/8 oz curd cheese

Put all the ingredients into a blender or food processor and work until you have a smooth soup. Put it into a saucepan and heat it gently to just below boiling point.

COURGETTE SCRAMBLE

450 g/1 lb courgettes
1 medium onion
25 g/1 oz butter
1 clove garlic, finely chopped
8 eggs
100 g/4 oz Cheddar cheese, grated
4 tablespoons chopped chervil or 2 tablespoons
  dried, or 4 tablespoons chopped parslsy
8 slices wholewheat toast, buttered if wished

Wipe and finely dice the courgettes. Melt the butter in a heavy saucepan on a low heat. Stir in the courgettes, onions and garlic. Cover and let them cook gently for 15 minutes. Beat the eggs with the cheese and chervil. Stir them into the courgettes. Keep the heat very low and stir continuously until the eggs are set, about 7 minutes. Either put all the scramble onto a serving plate or divide it between individual plates. Surround it with triangles of toast.

ANCHOVY OATCAKES WITH BLACK GRAPES

50 g/2 oz butter, softened
4 anchovy fillets
8 round oatcakes
8 black grapes
4 small bunches black grapes

Cream the butter. Chop and mash the anchovies and beat them into the butter. Spread the mixture over the oatcakes. Halve and seed the eight grapes. Arrange four halves in a star pattern on each oatcake. Put two oatcakes onto each of four small plates. Lay a small bunch of grapes beside them.

Corn and Vegetable Chowder
Cheese and Red Bean Salad
Rice, Celery and Carrot Salad
Stir-fried Apples with Toasted
Hazelnuts

CORN AND VEGETABLE CHOWDER

one 350-g/12-oz can sweetcorn
one 330-ml/11½-fl oz can tomato and
  vegetable juice
275 ml/½ pint single cream

Drain the sweetcorn. Put it into a saucepan with the vegetable juice and cream. Heat gently to just below boiling point.

CHEESE AND RED BEAN SALAD

one 400-g/14-oz can red kidney beans
225 g/8 oz Edam cheese
2 red peppers
2 ripe avocados
4 tablespoons natural yoghurt

Drain the beans. Dice the cheese. Core, seed and dice the peppers. Mix all these together. Halve, pit and peel the avocados. Mash them to a purée. Mix in the yoghurt. Fold the mixture into the beans, cheese and peppers.

RICE, CELERY AND CARROT SALAD

225 g/8 oz long-grain brown rice
¼ teaspoon salt
4 celery sticks
1 large carrot
4 tablespoons sunflower oil
2 tablespoons cider vinegar
1 clove garlic, crushed
freshly ground black pepper

Put the rice into a saucepan with 575 ml/1 pint cold water and the salt. Bring them to the boil, cover and simmer for 40 minutes or until the rice is tender and all the water absorbed. Turn the rice into a bowl. Finely chop the celery and grate the carrot. Add them to the rice. Beat together the oil, vinegar, garlic and pepper. Mix the resulting dressing into the rice.

STIR-FRIED APPLES WITH TOASTED HAZELNUTS

450 g/1 lb dessert apples
25 g/1 oz butter
1 teaspoon ground cinnamon
25 g/1 oz Barbados sugar
50 g/2 oz chopped toasted hazelnuts
single cream or natural yoghurt for serving
** (optional)**

Peel, core and slice the apples. Heat the butter in a large frying pan on a high heat. Put in the apples and stir them for 2 minutes or until they begin to soften. Stir in the cinnamon, sugar and hazelnuts. Keep the pan on the heat for a further 30 seconds. Serve the cream or yoghurt separately.

TUNA DIP WITH CRUDITÉS

one 200–g/7–oz can tuna fish
100 g/4 oz curd cheese or fromage blanc
grated rind and juice of ½ lemon
pinch of cayenne
3 small carrots
3 celery sticks
2 crisp dessert apples
4 black olives

Mash the tuna with its oil. Add the cheese and beat to make a smooth paste. Mix in the lemon rind and juice and cayenne. Cut the carrots and celery into matchstick pieces. Core the apples and cut each one into sixteen lengthways slices. Put a portion of the tuna dip into the centre of each of four small plates. Arrange some apple slices, celery pieces and carrot sticks around the edge of each plate. Pit and halve the olives and put two halves on top of each tuna dip.

PASTA WITH MOZARELLA CHEESE

225 g/8 oz pasta shapes
2 tablespoons olive oil
100 g/4 oz mozarella cheese, grated
4 tablespoons chopped parsley
freshly ground black pepper

Cook the pasta in lightly salted boiling water for 12 minutes or until it is tender. Drain it, run cold water through it and drain it again. Return it to the saucepan. Toss in the mozarella, parsley and plenty of pepper. Stir over a gentle heat to melt the cheese.

CANNELLINI BEANS WITH AUBERGINES

two 400-g/14-oz cans cannellini beans
450 g/1 lb aubergines
1 tablespoon salt
1 large onion
12 black olives
3 tablespoons olive oil
1 clove garlic, finely chopped
90 ml/3 fl oz tomato juice
1 tablespoon chopped thyme or
    1 teaspoon dried
1 tablespoon chopped marjoram or
    1 teaspoon dried

Drain the beans. Cut the aubergines into 1.5-cm/½-inch dice. Put them into a collander and sprinkle them with the salt. Leave them to drain for 10 minutes. Rinse them with cold water and dry them with absorbent kitchen paper. Thinly slice the onion. Pit and quarter the olives. Heat the oil in a saucepan on a low heat. Put in the onion and garlic and cook them for 2 minutes. Put in the aubergine, cover and cook for 5 minutes. Mix in the beans, olives, tomato juice and herbs. Cover and cook for 10 minutes.

STIR-FRIED ORANGES WITH DATES

4 medium oranges
100 g/4 oz pitted dates
40 g/1½ oz butter
2 tablespoons clear honey

Cut the rind and pith from the oranges. Thinly slice the flesh. Finely chop the dates. Melt the butter in a large frying pan on a high heat. Put in the oranges and stir them around for 1 minute so that they heat through but stay firm. Add the dates and honey. Cook for 30 seconds more.

Eggs Baked with Parsley and Capers
*Burghul Salad with Feta Cheese
and Hazelnuts*
Gingered Pears

EGGS BAKED WITH PARSLEY AND CAPERS

4 eggs
25 g/1 oz butter
4 tablespoons chopped parsley
4 tablespoons chopped capers
freshly ground black pepper
4 tablespoons double cream

Heat the oven to 180°C, 350°F, gas 4. Put a knob of butter into the bottom of each of four individual soufflé dishes. Stand the dishes on a baking sheet and put them into the oven for the butter to melt. Take out the dishes. Stir 1 tablespoon parsley and 1 tablespoon capers into each dish. Break an egg on top and season it with pepper. Spoon 1 tablespoon double cream over each yolk. Bake the eggs for 15 minutes until the whites are set but the yolks still soft.

BURGHUL SALAD WITH FETA CHEESE AND HAZELNUTS

wheat salad:
225 g/8 oz burghul wheat★
1 red pepper
1 green pepper
4 tablespoons olive oil
2 tablespoons white wine vinegar
1 clove garlic, crushed

cheese and hazelnut salad:
175 g/6 oz feta cheese★★
100 g/4 oz hazelnuts
450 g/1 lb tomatoes
2 tablespoons olive oil
1 tablespoon white wine vinegar
2 tablespoons chopped basil or 1 teaspoon dried

Put the wheat into a bowl. Pour boiling water over it and leave it for 5 minutes. Drain it and squeeze it dry. Core, seed and dice the peppers. Add them to the wheat. Beat the remaining ingredients together to make the dressing. Fold them into the wheat.

Dice the cheese and chop the tomatoes. Mix these with the hazelnuts. Beat together the oil and vinegar. Mix in the basil. Fold the dressing into the cheese, hazelnuts and tomatoes.

Put a ring of the wheat salad round the edge of a serving plate. Arrange the cheese and hazelnut salad in the centre.

*Burghul wheat is a soaked and precooked wheat, taking the form of small yellow grains. It can be bought in health food shops. It is usually soaked in warm water, but boiling water speeds up the process.

**Feta cheese is a light textured, white cheese made in Greece. It is usually vacuum packed and can be bought in most supermarkets.

GINGERED PEARS

450 g/1 lb firm pears
4 pieces preserved stem ginger, chopped
25 g/1 oz butter
½ teaspoon ground ginger
½ teaspoon ground coriander
2 tablespoons syrup from the ginger jar

Peel and core the pears. Cut them into pieces about 3 cm/1½ inches long and 1.5 cm/½ inch square. Heat the butter in a large frying pan on a high heat. Put in the pieces of pear and stir-fry them for 1 minute. Sprinkle in the spices and add the ginger and syrup. Stir for a further 30 seconds. Serve as soon as possible.

Carrot and Tomato Juice Appetiser
Brown Rice with Chicken Livers
Spring Greens with Onions
Grilled Bananas with Raisin Sauce

CARROT AND TOMATO JUICE APPETISER

400 ml/14 fl oz carrot juice
200 ml/7 fl oz tomato juice
4 tablespoons vodka (optional)
1 teaspoon Tabasco sauce

Pour the carrot and tomato juices and vodka into a jug and stir well to make sure that they are evenly mixed. Serve in wine glasses.

BROWN RICE WITH CHICKEN LIVERS

450 g/1 lb chicken livers
225 g/8 oz courgettes
1 large onion
25 g/1 oz butter
1 clove garlic, finely chopped
225 g/8 oz long-grain brown rice
pinch of saffron or 1 teaspoon ground turmeric
575 ml/1 pint stock

Finely chop the chicken livers, courgettes and onion. Melt the butter in a saucepan on a low heat. Put in the onion and garlic and soften them. Raise the heat. Put in the chicken livers and stir for 2 minutes to brown them. Lower the heat again. Stir in the rice, courgettes, and saffron or turmeric. Pour in the stock and bring it to the boil. Cover and cook on a low heat for 40 minutes or until the rice is tender and most of the stock has been absorbed.

SPRING GREENS WITH ONIONS

675 g/1½ lb spring greens
1 large onion, thinly sliced
1 clove garlic, finely chopped
25 g/1 oz butter
175 ml/6 fl oz stock

Wash and chop the spring greens. Melt the butter in a saucepan on a low heat. Put in the onion and garlic and soften them. Raise the heat to moderate. Stir in the greens. Pour in the stock and bring it to the boil. Cover and cook on a moderate heat for 20 minutes, by which time most of the water should be evaporated and the leaves should be bright and shiny.

GRILLED BANANAS WITH RAISIN SAUCE

4 bananas
butter for greasing
juice of ½ lemon
4 tablespoons Barbados sugar

sauce:
200 ml/7 fl oz natural orange juice
grated rind of ½ lemon
100 g/4 oz raisins

Peel the bananas and cut them in half lengthways. Put them, cut side up, into a shallow, flameproof serving dish. Pour the lemon juice over them. Heat the grill to high. Put the bananas under the grill for 2 minutes. Turn them and sprinkle them with the sugar. Grill them for a further 2 minutes.

For the sauce, put all the ingredients into a saucepan, bring them to the boil and simmer them for 2 minutes. Pour the sauce over the bananas and serve straight from the dish.

Sesame Seed Salad
Mixed Macaroni Cheese
Pineapple Rings Topped with
Almonds

SESAME SEED SALAD

100 g/ 4 oz watercress
450 g/ 1 lb tomatoes
100 g/4 oz button mushrooms
50 g/2 oz currants
4 tablespoons sunflower oil
2 tablespoons cider vinegar
1 teaspoon Dijon mustard
1 clove garlic, crushed
4 tablespoons sesame seeds

Chop the watercress and tomatoes and thinly slice the mushrooms. Mix them together and divide them between four small serving bowls. Mix one quarter of the currants into each portion of salad. Beat the oil, vinegar, mustard and garlic together to make the dressing. Fold a little into each bowl. Scatter the sesame seeds over the top.

MIXED MACARONI CHEESE

1 large cauliflower
1 bay leaf
225 g/8 oz wholewheat macaroni
4 rashers rindless back bacon
25 g/1 oz butter
3 tablespoons wholewheat flour
425 ml/³⁄₄ pint milk
2 teaspoons made English mustard
½ teaspoon dried sage
150 g/5 oz Cheddar cheese, grated
one 400-g/14-oz can butter beans, drained

Heat the oven to 200°C, 400°F, gas 6. Cut the cauliflower into small florets. Steam them, with the bay leaf, for 15 minutes, or until they are just tender. Cook the macaroni in lightly salted boiling water for 12 minutes. Drain it, run cold water through it and drain it again. Grill and chop the bacon. Melt the butter in a saucepan on a medium heat. Stir in the flour and then the milk. Bring the sauce to the boil, stirring. Simmer for 2 minutes. Take the pan from the heat. Beat in the mustard, sage and three-quarters of the cheese. Fold in the cauliflower, macaroni, bacon and beans. Put the mixture into an ovenproof dish. Scatter the remaining cheese over the top. Put the dish into the oven for 15 minutes.

PINEAPPLE RINGS TOPPED WITH ALMONDS

1 large pineapple
100 g/4 oz ground almonds
125 ml/4 fl oz concentrated apple juice★
10 glacé cherries

Cut the husk from the pineapple. Cut the flesh into eight rings. Cut away the centre core. Put the pineapple rings into a shallow, flameproof dish and spoon over half the concentrated apple juice. Mix together the almonds and remaining apple juice. Finely chop six of the cherries and incorporate them into the mixture.

Heat the grill to high. Grill the pineapple rings for 2 minutes, or until they are beginning to brown. Turn them and grill them for 1 minute. Put a portion of the almond mixture on top of each pineapple slice. Top it with half a glacé cherry. Return the pineapple to the grill for 2 minutes, or until the almond mixture is lightly browned.

★Concentrated apple juice is a sweet, dark brown syrup that can be bought from health food shops.

> *Grilled Courgette Slices*
> *Pasta with Leeks and Two Cheeses*
> *Iceberg Salad*
> *Mixed Fruit Kissel*

GRILLED COURGETTE SLICES

450 g/1 lb small courgettes
25 g/1 oz butter, melted
about 1 tablespoon spiced granular mustard

Heat the grill to high. Cut the courgettes each into four thin lengthways slices. Brush them with the melted butter. Grill the courgette slices for about 3 minutes or until one side is golden brown. (Note: place any end pieces skin side up for this first grilling.) Turn the slices and spread them with the mustard. Grill for 3 minutes, or until the second side is brown.

PASTA WITH LEEKS AND TWO CHEESES

225 g/8 oz wholewheat pasta
450 g/1 lb leeks
75 g/3 oz Lymeswold or blue Brie cheese
75 g/3 oz Melbury or Brie cheese
25 g/1 oz butter
100 g/4 oz chopped mixed nuts
4 tablespoons chopped parsley

Cook the pasta in lightly salted boiling water for 12 minutes or until it is just tender. Drain it, run cold water through it and drain it again. While the pasta is cooking, thinly slice the leeks. Finely dice the cheeses. Melt the butter in a saucepan on a low heat. Stir in the leeks, cover them and cook them gently for 10 minutes. Mix in the pasta, cheeses, nuts and parsley. Stir on a low heat until the cheeses begin to melt and the mixture is heated through.

ICEBERG SALAD

1 iceberg lettuce
1 large red pepper
1 large orange
4 tablespoons olive oil
2 tablespoons white wine vinegar
1 clove garlic, crushed
pinch of cayenne
1 tablespoon tomato purée

Shred the lettuce. Core and seed the pepper and cut it into pieces about 6 mm × 2 cm/¼ × ¾ inch. Cut the rind and pith from the orange. Cut the flesh into lengthways quarters and thinly slice them. In a salad bowl, mix the lettuce, pepper and orange. Beat the remaining ingredients together to make the dressing. Fold it into the salad.

MIXED FRUIT KISSEL

A kissel is a fruit soup. Usually, it is served chilled, but if time is limited it can also be served hot or warm.

one 370-g/13-oz can raspberries in natural juice
one 213-g/7 ½-oz can blackberries in
**   natural juice**
one 213-g/7 ½-oz can blackcurrants in
**   natural juice**
50 g/2 oz honey
2 tablespoons arrowroot or cornflour
150 ml/¼ pint soured cream

Rub all the fruits with their juices through a sieve. Reserve 125 ml/4 fl oz and put the rest into a saucepan. Add the honey. Stir on a low heat for the honey to dissolve. Bring the fruit purée to just below boiling point. Put the arrowroot or cornflour into a bowl. Stir in the reserved purée to make a smooth paste. Stir the paste into the saucepan. Bring the mixture to the boil and stir with a wooden spoon until it thickens. Pour the kissel into individual bowls. Serve hot or warm or chilled, with a portion of soured cream floating on the top.

Prawn and Parsley Salad
Tomato and
Mushroom Pancakes
Apricot and Chocolate Trifles

PRAWN AND PARSLEY SALAD

225 g/8 oz shelled prawns
15 g/½ oz parsley, chopped
4 tablespoons olive oil
juice of ½ lemon
1 teaspoon paprika
1 clove garlic, crushed
4 thin lemon slices

Mix together the prawns and parsley. Beat together the remaining ingredients and fold them into the prawns. Divide the salad between four small dishes. Garnish each one with a twist of lemon.

TOMATO AND MUSHROOM PANCAKES

batter:
100 g/4 oz wholewheat flour
pinch of salt
½ teaspoon dried thyme
1 egg
1 egg yolk
1 tablespoon tomato purée
150 ml/¼ pint milk
150 ml/¼ pint water
1 tablespoon sunflower oil plus extra for frying

filling:
450 g/1 lb ripe tomatoes
225 g/8 oz open mushrooms
6 black olives (optional)
2 tablespoons olive or sunflower oil
1 large onion, finely chopped
1 clove garlic, finely chopped
1 tablespoon chopped marjoram or
   1 teaspoon dried
1 tablespoon tomato purée
175 g/6 oz Edam cheese

For the pancakes, put the flour, salt and thyme into a mixing bowl and make a well in the centre. Put in the egg, egg yolk and tomato purée and gradually begin to beat in flour from the sides of the well. Mix together the milk and water. Gradually beat in half the mixture into the flour. Beat in the oil and then the remaining milk and water mixture. Leave the mixture in a cool place while you prepare the filling.

Scald, skin and chop the tomatoes. Finely chop the mushrooms. Pit and chop the olives. Heat the oil in a frying pan on a low heat. Put in the onion and garlic and soften them. Raise the heat to medium. Put in the mushrooms and cook them for 2 minutes, stirring. Mix in the tomatoes, marjoram and tomato purée. Lower the heat and simmer for 2 minutes, uncovered, until the mixture becomes thick. Take the pan from the heat and mix in the olives.

Fry the pancakes, using 3 tablespoons mixture for each one, to make eight in all. Grate the cheese. Roll up a portion of the tomato mixture in each pancake. Lay the pancakes on a flameproof serving dish. Scatter the cheese over the top. Put the dish under a high grill for the cheese to melt.

APRICOT AND CHOCOLATE TRIFLES

one 425-g/15-oz can apricots in natural juice
20 ratafias
350 g/12 oz chocolate soya dessert★

Drain the apricots, reserving the juice. Cut four of the apricot halves into quarters and reserve them. Halve the rest. Crumble four ratafias into the base of each of four glass dishes. Spoon 2 tablespoons of the reserved juice over them. If possible, leave them for 15 minutes. Put in the halved apricot pieces and cover them with the chocolate dessert. Garnish each dish with a whole ratafia and four thin slices of apricot.

★Soya dessert is a type of soya milk blancmange made with only natural ingredients and raw sugar. It can be bought from most health food shops.

> *Carrot and Raisin Cheese*
> *Corn and Tuna Pancake Stack*
> *Stir-fried Spinach*
> *Maple Syrup Fruit Salad*

CARROT AND RAISIN CHEESE

225 g/8 oz carrots
50 g/2 oz raisins
100 g/4 oz cottage cheese
1 tablespoon poppy seeds
2 tablespoons white wine vinegar
watercress for garnish

Grate the carrots. Mix together the carrots, raisins, cheese, poppy seeds and vinegar. Put a portion of the mixture in the centre of each of four small plates. Arrange watercress sprigs round it and put one watercress leaf on top.

CORN AND TUNA PANCAKE STACK

batter:
50 g/2 oz wholewheat flour
50 g/2 oz cornmeal★
1 teaspoon paprika
pinch of salt
1 egg
1 egg yolk
150 ml/¼ pint milk
150 ml/¼ pint water
1 tablespoon corn or sunflower oil

filling:
one 200-g/7-oz can tuna
one 350-g/12-oz can sweetcorn
1 medium onion
25 g/1 oz butter
3 tablespoons wholewheat flour
275 ml/½ pint milk
4 tablespoons chopped parsley
grated rind of 1 lemon
freshly ground black pepper
350 g/12 oz tomatoes

To make the batter, put the flour, cornmeal, paprika and salt into a bowl and make a well in the centre. Put in the egg and egg yolk and gradually begin to beat in flour from the sides of the well. Mix together the milk and water. Beat half the mixture into the flour. Beat in the oil and then the remaining milk and water mixture. Leave the batter in a cool place while you prepare the filling.

Drain and flake the tuna. Drain the sweetcorn. Thinly slice the onion. Melt the butter in a saucepan on a low heat. Put in the onion and soften it. Stir in the flour and then the milk. Bring the sauce to the boil, stirring. Simmer it for 2 minutes. Put in the corn, tuna, parsley and lemon rind. Season with the pepper and stir to heat through.

Fry the pancakes, using 3 tablespoons mixture for each. Then put a pancake onto a flameproof serving plate and spread some of the corn mixture on top. Continue layering to use up all the pancakes and filling. There will be a layer of filling on top. Slice the tomatoes and arrange them over the filling. Put the dish under a high grill for 2 minutes for the tomatoes to heat through. Serve by cutting into quarters.

Cornmeal is a coarse, pale yellow flour produced by grinding sweetcorn kernels. It can be bought from health food shops, delicatessens and some supermarkets.

STIR-FRIED SPINACH

two 300 g/10 oz packs frozen spinach, thawed
25 g/1 oz butter or vegetable margarine
1 small onion, thinly sliced
¼ nutmeg, grated, or ¼ teaspoon ground
   nutmeg

Chop the spinach. Melt the butter or margarine in a large frying pan on a high heat. Put in the spinach and onion and stir-fry them for 2 minutes. Grate in the nutmeg. Take the pan from the heat and serve as soon as possible.

MAPLE SYRUP FRUIT SALAD

1 small honeydew melon
2 Cox apples
2 pink grapefruit
8 tablespoons maple syrup
4 pecan halves or walnut halves
2 tablespoons chopped pecan nuts or walnuts

Halve the melon. Remove the seeds. Cut the melon into slices and cut away the rind. Dice the slices. Core and dice the apples. Cut the rind and pith from the grapefruit. Cut the fruit in half lengthways and then into thin crossways slices. Arrange a ring of grapefruit slices round the edge of four small plates. Spoon 1 tablespoon maple syrup over the top. Put the melon and apple into a bowl and mix them with the remaining maple syrup. Put a portion of the melon and apple into the centre of the grapefruit. Top it with a pecan or walnut half. Scatter the chopped pecans or walnuts over the grapefruit.

MICROWAVE RECIPES

If you own a microwave oven, you will be able to cook some types of dishes and cuts of meat in less than half the time that they would take in a conventional oven and without having to wait for the cooker to come up to temperature. The cooking times given below should be right for most makes of microwave oven, but if you have any queries, consult the manufacturer's instructions.

POTS OF CORN AND CHEESE

one 350-g/12-oz can sweetcorn kernels
100 g/4 oz Cheddar cheese, grated
4 tablespoons natural yoghurt
2 teaspoons paprika
¼ teaspoon chilli powder
4 tablespoons chopped parsley

Drain the corn. Mix it with three-quarters of the cheese and all the remaining ingredients. Divide the mixture between four small soufflé dishes. Scatter the remaining cheese over the top. Cook in the micro-wave oven on high for 4 minutes.

HOT AVOCADOS WITH PARSLEY SALAD

2 ripe avocados
2 tablespoons olive oil
1 tablespoon red wine vinegar
½ teaspoon Dijon mustard
1 clove garlic, crushed
25 g/1 oz parsley, chopped

Halve and pit the avocados. Put each half onto an individual dish. Beat together the oil, vinegar, mustard and garlic. Mix in the parsley. Fill the centres of the avocados with the Parsley mixture. Cover the avocados with cling film. Cook all the dishes together in the microwave oven on high for 2 minutes. Serve hot.

SPICED BEEF LOAF WITH YOGHURT SAUCE

675 g/1½ lb minced beef
1 tablespoon chopped thyme, or 1 teaspoon
** dried**
4 sage leaves, chopped, or ½ teaspoon dried
** sage**
1 teaspoon ground cinnamon
2 tablespoons tomato purée
2 tablespoons natural yoghurt
25 g/1 oz butter
1 large onion, finely chopped
1 clove garlic, finely chopped

sauce:
150 ml/¼ pint natural yoghurt
1 teaspoon ground cinnamon
1 tablespoon tomato purée

Put the beef into a large mixing bowl with the thyme, sage, cinnamon, tomato purée and yoghurt. Beat them together well. Melt the butter in a frying pan on a low heat, put in the onion and garlic and soften them. Add them to the beef and mix well. Put the mixture into a 900 g/2 lb microwave-proof loaf dish. Cover and cook in the microwave oven on high for 12 minutes. Let the loaf stand for 10 minutes. Turn it out and cut it into thick slices for serving.

Make the sauce while the loaf is cooking. Put the yoghurt into a bowl and beat in the remaining ingredients to make a smooth mixture. Serve the sauce separately.

PEANUT CHICKEN WITH PINEAPPLE

**one 1.575-kg/3½-lb roasting chicken, or 4
  chicken joints**
2 tablespoons peanut butter
2 tablespoons tomato purée
4 tablespoons pineapple juice
1 teaspoon curry powder
1 teaspoon paprika
4 slices pineapple, fresh or canned in juice

Joint the chicken. Mix together the peanut butter, tomato purée, pineapple juice, curry powder and paprika. Spread the mixture over the chicken joints. Lay the chicken pieces on a microwave-proof dish with the thicker parts pointing outwards. Chop two of the pineapple rings and scatter the pieces over the chicken. Cover and cook in the microwave oven on high for 15 minutes. Cover the bone ends and wing tips with small pieces of foil. Cover and cook in the microwave oven on high for a further 5 minutes. Cut the remaining slices of pineapple in half. Place a half on each chicken portion. Cover and cook in the microwave oven on high for a further 2 minutes. Let stand, covered, for 10 minutes before serving.

POTATO, HAM AND APPLE LAYER

675 g/1½ lb potatoes
350 g/12 oz cooked lean ham
2 medium cooking apples
25 g/1 oz butter
2 medium onions, thinly sliced
freshly ground black pepper
4 sage leaves, chopped
4 tablespoons chopped parsley
200 ml/7 fl oz stock
200 ml/7 fl oz dry cider
150 ml/¼ pint soured cream

Scrub and thinly slice the potatoes. Dice the ham. Peel, core and slice the apples. Put the onions into a bowl with the butter. Cover them with cling film or a lid. Cook in the microwave oven on high for 4 minutes. Layer the potatoes, apple, ham and onion in a deep, microwave-proof dish, seasoning and adding the herbs as you go and ending with a layer of potatoes. Pour in the stock and cider. Cover and cook in the microwave oven on high for 25 minutes. Spoon the soured cream over the top. Cover again. Cook in the microwave oven on high for 2 minutes.

COD TOPPED WITH CHEESE AND WORCESTERSHIRE SAUCE

675 g/1½ lb cod fillet
butter for greasing
juice of 1 lemon
salt and freshly ground black pepper
125 g/4 oz Cheddar cheese, grated
2 tablespoons Worcestershire sauce
3 tablespoons chopped parsley

Skin the cod and cut it into pieces 7.5-10 cm/3-4 inches square. Lay the pieces in a buttered, micro-wave-proof dish. Sprinkle over the lemon juice and pepper. Leave it for 10 minutes. Mix together the cheese, Worcestershire sauce and parsley. Dot the mixture on top of the fish. Cover with cling film or a lid. Cook in the microwave oven on high for 8 minutes. Let dish stand for 4 minutes before serving.

EGGS BAKED WITH TUNA FISH

4 eggs
one 200-g/7-oz can tuna fish
2 large onions
4 tablespoons olive oil
1 clove garlic, chopped
16 green olives
¼ teaspoon cayenne
4 tablespoons chopped parsley

Thinly slice the onions. Put them into a bowl with the oil and garlic. Cover them with cling film or a lid. Cook in the microwave oven on high for 4 minutes. While the onions are cooking, drain and flake the tuna and pit and quarter the olives. Mix together the onions and garlic, tuna, cayenne and parsley, olives. Put them into a 20- or 23-cm/8- or 9-inch diameter, shallow microwave-proof dish. Make four indentations in the mixture with the back of a tablespoon. Break an egg into each indentation. Cover with cling film or a lid. Cook in the microwave oven on high for 5 minutes, checking at 4 minutes. Allow to stand for 2 minutes before serving.

HONEYED PEACH AND WALNUT PUDDING

two 213-g/7 ½-oz cans peach slices in fruit juice
125 g/4 oz wholewheat flour
1 teaspoon bicarbonate of soda
4 tablespoons corn oil
2 eggs, beaten
125 g/4 oz honey, melted
175 g/3 oz walnuts, chopped

Drain one of the cans of peaches and reserve the juice. Put the peaches into the bottom of a 23-cm/9-inch diameter microwave-proof tart dish. Add the other peaches and their juice. Put the flour and bicarbonate of soda into a mixing bowl. make a well in the centre. Gradually beat in the oil, eggs and 4 tablespoons of the reserved juice. Then beat in the honey to make a thick batter. Fold in the walnuts. Spoon the mixture over the peach slices. Cook in the microwave oven on high for 16 minutes. Let stand for 10 minutes before serving straight from the dish.

CREAMY KIWI FRUIT LAYER

5 kiwi fruit
100 g/4 oz crunchy oat cereal
250 ml/8 fl oz double cream

Peel the kiwi fruit. Finely chop four. Cut the fifth into four slices. Use small, microwave-proof dishes. Into each one put 15 g/½ oz of the oat cereal. Scatter half a chopped kiwi fruit over the top and spoon over 2 tablespoons double cream. Repeat the layers. Cook all the dishes together in a microwave oven for 2 minutes. Put a slice of kiwi fruit on top of each one. Cook in the microwave oven for a further half minute. Serve hot.

APPLES FILLED WITH COCONUT

4 large cooking apples
75 g/3 oz dessicated coconut
1 egg yolk
4 tablespoons concentrated apple juice
150 ml/ ¼ pint water
2 glacé cherries

Core the apples and score them round the middle. Put them onto a microwave-proof dish. Mix the coconut with the egg yolk and 4 tablespoons of the concentrated apple juice. Fill the apples with the mixture. Mix the remaining concentrated apple juice with the water and pour it round the apples. Top each apple with a cherry half. Cook in the microwave oven on high for 10 minutes.

PRESSURE-COOKED DISHES

A pressure cooker is ideal for quickly making dishes that otherwise would have to be simmered or boiled for a considerable time on top of the stove or cooked slowly in the oven. These include soups, stews and casseroles, dishes made from dried pulses, steamed puddings and poached dried fruits. When making dishes with pulses, remember that the pulses should be soaked before being cooked. The method for using different types of pressure cooker varies slightly, so if you have any queries, consult the manufacturer's instructions.

BORSCHT

(A soup for a first course)

450 g/1 lb raw beetroot
225 g/8 oz carrots
225 g/8 oz white cabbage
4 tomatoes
1 large onion
850 ml/1½ pints stock
4 tablespoons red wine vinegar
2 tablespoons tomato purée
1 teaspoon Barbados sugar
1 clove garlic, crushed with pinch of salt
freshly ground black pepper
bouquet garni
4 tablespoons chopped parsley
4 tablespoons soured cream

Peel the beetroot and cut them into matchstick pieces. Cut the carrots in the same way. Finely shred the cabbage. Scald, skin and chop the tomatoes. Thinly slice the onion. Put the stock into the pressure cooker and bring it to the boil. Add all the other ingredients except the parsley and soured cream. Put the lid on the cooker. Bring it up to pressure and cook for 10 minutes. Release the steam quickly. Ladle the soup into individual bowls. Scatter the parsley over the top and put a portion of soured cream in the centre of each bowl.

RED LENTIL AND LEMON SOUP

175 g/6 oz red lentils
½ lemon
2 medium onions
3 tablespoons sunflower oil
1 clove garlic, chopped
2 teaspoons curry powder
850 ml/1½ pints stock
1 bay leaf
5-cm/2-inch cinnamon stick
4 cloves

Thinly slice the lemon and finely chop the onions. Heat the oil in the pressure cooker on a low heat. Put in the onions and garlic and soften them. Stir in the curry powder and lentils and stir for 1 minute. Pour in the stock and bring it to the boil. Add the lemon, bay leaf, cinnamon stick and cloves. Put the lid on the cooker and bring it up to pressure. Cook for 5 minutes. Release the steam slowly. Remove the lemon slices, bay leaf and cinnamon stick before serving the soup.

CURRANTY BEEF AND CARROTS

675 g/1½ lb braising steak, sliced, or beef skirt
675 g/1½ lb carrots
50 g/2 oz currants
2 large onions, thinly sliced
6 tablespoons chopped parsley
6 allspice berries, crushed
salt and freshly ground black pepper
850 ml/1½ pints stock
bouquet garni

Cut the beef into pieces about 2.5 × 5 cm/1 × 2 inches. Slice the carrots. Layer the beef, carrots, currants and onions in a pressure cooker, scattering them with the parsley, allspice, a little salt and a liberal amount of pepper. Pour in the stock and put in the bouquet garni. Bring the contents of the cooker to the boil. Put on the lid and bring the cooker up to pressure. Cook for 10 minutes. Release the steam slowly.

LAMB AND PASTA GOULASH

675 g/1½ lb lean lamb
225 g/8 oz mushrooms
2 medium onions
3 tablespoons sunflower oil
1 clove garlic, finely chopped
1 tablespoon paprika
1 teaspoon caraway seeds
850 ml/1½ pints stock
225 g/8 oz wholewheat pasta shapes
1 bay leaf
150 ml/¼ pint soured cream
4 tablespoons chopped parsley

Cut the lamb into 2.5-cm/1-inch cubes. Thinly slice the mushrooms and onions. Heat the oil in a pressure cooker on a high heat. Put in the lamb, brown it quickly and remove it. Lower the heat. Put in the onions and garlic and cook them for 2 minutes. Stir in the paprika and caraway seeds. Cook until the onions are soft. Pour in the stock and bring it to the boil. Put in the lamb, pasta shapes, mushrooms and bay leaf. Cover the pressure cooker and bring it up to pressure. Cook for 10 minutes. Release the pressure slowly. Take off the lid and stir in the soured cream. Serve scattered with the parsley.

BRAISED CHICKEN AND CELERY WITH ANCHOVIES

one 1.575 kg/3½ lb roasting chicken
one small head celery
1 large onion
4 anchovy fillets
150 ml/¼ pint stock
15 g/½ oz butter
150 ml/¼ pint dry white wine
3 chopped sage leaves or ½ teaspoon dried
1 tablespoon chopped thyme or 1 teaspoon dried

Joint the chicken. Cut the celery into 2.5-cm/1-inch pieces. Thinly slice the onion. Mash the anchovy fillets to a paste and mix them with the stock. Heat the butter in a pressure cooker on a medium heat. Put in the chicken pieces, brown them and remove them. Lower the heat. Put in the onion and celery. Balance the lid on the cooker but do not seal it. Cook the onion and celery for 5 minutes. Pour in the stock and wine and bring them to the boil. Add the herbs and replace the chicken. Cover the cooker and bring it up to pressure. Cook for 5 minutes, then release the steam quickly.

BLACK-EYED BEAN AND VEGETABLE CURRY

225 g/8 oz black-eyed beans, soaked and
  drained
225 g/8 oz carrots
225 g/8 oz potatoes
2 green peppers
1 aubergine
4 green or red chillies★
2 medium onions
25 g/1 oz fresh root ginger★★
3 tablespoons sunflower oil
2 cloves garlic, chopped
1 teaspoon curry powder
1 teaspoon ground turmeric
725 ml/1¼ pints stock
50 g/2 oz creamed coconut★★★
1 bay leaf

Slice the carrots. Scrub and dice the potatoes. Core
and seed the peppers and cut them into 2.5-cm/1-inch
squares. Cut the aubergine into 2.5-cm/1-inch dice.
Core, seed and chop the chillies. Thinly slice the
onions. Peel and grate the root ginger.

Heat the oil in a pressure cooker on a low heat. Put
in the onions, garlic, chillies and ginger. Cook them
for 2 minutes. Stir in the curry powder and turmeric.
Cook until the onions are soft. Pour in the stock and
bring it to the boil. Put in the creamed coconut and
stir until it melts. Drain the beans and put them into
the pressure cooker together with the carrots,
peppers, aubergines and potatoes. Put on the lid and
bring the cooker up to pressure. Cook for 6 minutes.
Release the steam slowly before opening. Remove
the bay leaf before serving.

★*If no fresh chillies are available, use ¼ teaspoon chilli
powder. Add it with the curry powder.*

★★*If fresh ginger is not available, use 1 teaspoon ground
ginger. Add it with the curry powder.*

★★★*Creamed coconut comes in 200 g/7 oz blocks and can be
bought from delicatessens, Indian shops, health food shops
and most supermarkets.*

RED BEANS WITH CHEESY VEGETABLE RICE

225 g/8 oz red kidney beans, soaked and drained
2 red peppers
125 g/4 oz mushrooms
225 g/8 oz courgettes
1 medium onion
3 tablespoons sunflower oil
1 clove garlic, chopped
225 g/8 oz long-grain brown rice
725 ml/1¼ pints stock
1 tablespoon chopped thyme
pinch of salt
freshly ground black pepper
2 tablespoons soy sauce
125 g/4 oz Red Leicester cheese, grated
4 tablespoons chopped parsley

Core, seed and chop the peppers. Chop the mushrooms, courgettes and onion. Heat the oil in a pressure cooker on a low heat. Put in the onion and garlic and soften them. Stir in the rice and vegetables. Pour in the stock and bring it to the boil. Add the thyme, seasoning and soy sauce. Put in the beans. Cover the cooker and bring it up to pressure. Cook for 10 minutes. Release the steam slowly. Fork in the cheese and the parsley just before serving. No accompaniment is needed.

SPICED GREEN LENTILS WITH WHEAT

175 g/6 oz green lentils
175 g/6 oz burghul wheat★
225 g/8 oz carrots
4 celery sticks
2 medium onions
3 tablespoons sunflower oil
1 clove garlic, chopped
2 teaspoons cumin seeds
2 teaspoons ground coriander
275 ml/½ pint tomato juice
850 ml/1½ pints stock
¼ teaspoon salt
freshly ground black pepper
4 tablespoons chopped parsley

Finely chop the carrots, celery and onions. Heat the oil in a pressure cooker on a low heat. Put in the onions and garlic and cook them for 2 minutes. Stir in the cumin seeds and ground coriander, carrots and celery. Pour in the tomato juice and stock and bring them to the boil. Put in the lentils and wheat and seasonings. Cover the cooker and bring it up to pressure. Cook for 15 minutes. Release the steam slowly. Stir in the parsley just before serving.

★*Burghul wheat is a pre-cooked, cracked wheat which can be bought from health food shops.*

FIGS IN WINE

450 g/1 lb dried figs
thinly pared rind of 1 large orange
7.5-cm/3-inch cinnamon stick
150 ml/¼ pint dry red wine
275 ml/½ pint natural orange juice

Put the figs into the pressure cooker. Cut the orange rind into thin slivers and add it to the figs with the cinnamon stick. Put the wine and orange juice into a saucepan and bring them to the boil. Pour them over the figs. Let figs soak for 10 minutes. Put the lid on the cooker and bring it up to pressure. Cook for 10 minutes. Release the steam slowly. Serve hot or cold.

PEARS IN CIDER WITH HONEY CUSTARD

4 large, firm pears
150 ml/¼ pint dry cider
⅛ nutmeg, freshly grated, or ¼ teaspoon
    ground nutmeg
2 tablespoons clear honey

custard:
2 eggs
2 tablespoons clear honey
three drops vanilla essence
425 ml/¾ pint milk
butter or vegetable margarine for greasing
⅛ nutmeg, freshly grated, or ¼ teaspoon
    ground nutmeg

for cooking:
juice of ½ lemon

Peel, core and slice the pears. Put them into a dish with the cider. Grate in the nutmeg and spoon in the honey. Cover with greaseproof paper and tie it down.

For the custard, beat the eggs with the honey and vanilla essence. Gently warm the milk and stir it into the eggs. Pour the mixture into a greased dish and sprinkle the top with nutmeg. Cover with greaseproof paper and tie it down.

Put 275 ml/½ pint water and the lemon juice into the bottom of a pressure cooker. Put the dish of fruit into the cooker. Lay the pressure cooker trivet on top and put the dish of custard on top of that. Put the lid on the cooker. Bring the cooker up to pressure and cook for 15 minutes. Release the steam slowly.

APRICOT RICE

This is much darker and far more tasty than an ordinary rice pudding.

100 g/4 oz dried whole apricots
15 g/½ oz butter
575 ml/1 pint milk
50 g/2 oz short-grain brown rice
grated rind of 1 medium orange
25 g/1 oz Barbados suar

Quarter the apricots. Put them into a bowl, pour boiling water over them and leave them for 5 minutes. Drain them. Put the butter into the pressure cooker and melt it on a low heat. Put in the milk and bring it to the boil. Add the rice. Stir until the milk begins to boil up the sides of the cooker. Lower the heat and wait until the milk settles to a rolling boil in the bottom of the cooker. Add the apricots and orange rind. Put on the lid. Bring the cooker up to pressure. Cook for 12 minutes. Release the steam slowly. Stir in the sugar.

INDEX